STATE PROFILES

OKLAHOMA

BY COLLEEN SEXTON

BELLWETHER MEDIA • MINNEAPOLIS, MN

Blastoff! Discovery launches a new mission: reading to learn. Filled with facts and features, each book offers you an exciting new world to explore!

BLASTOFF! UNIVERSE

BLASTOFF! Beginners — GRADE K

BLASTOFF! READERS — GRADES 1-3

DISCOVERY — GRADE 4

This edition first published in 2022 by Bellwether Media, Inc.

No part of this publication may be reproduced in whole or in part without written permission of the publisher.
For information regarding permission, write to Bellwether Media, Inc.,
Attention: Permissions Department,
6012 Blue Circle Drive, Minnetonka, MN 55343.

Library of Congress Cataloging-in-Publication Data

Names: Sexton, Colleen A., 1967- author.
Title: Oklahoma / by Colleen Sexton.
Description: Minneapolis, MN : Bellwether Media, Inc., 2022. |
   Series: Blastoff! Discovery: State profiles | Includes bibliographical
   references and index. | Audience: Ages 7-13 | Audience: Grades
   4-6 | Summary: "Engaging images accompany information about
   Oklahoma. The combination of high-interest subject matter and
   narrative text is intended for students in grades 3 through
   8"– Provided by publisher.
Identifiers: LCCN 2021020858 (print) | LCCN 2021020859
   (ebook) | ISBN 9781644873410 (library binding) | ISBN
   9781648341847 (ebook)
Subjects: LCSH: Oklahoma–Juvenile literature.
Classification: LCC F694.3 .S48 2022 (print) | LCC F694.3 (ebook)
   | DDC 976.6–dc23
LC record available at https://lccn.loc.gov/2021020858
LC ebook record available at https://lccn.loc.gov/2021020859

Editor: Rebecca Sabelko   Designer: Kathleen Petelinsek

Printed in the United States of America, North Mankato, MN.

TABLE OF CONTENTS

Road trip! A family is driving along Route 66 through Oklahoma. They are visiting some of this historic highway's offbeat sights. The family stops at the world's tallest concrete **totem pole** in Chelsea. It rises 90 feet (27 meters) tall! Next is the Blue Whale of Catoosa. The family enters the giant whale sculpture through its wide-open mouth.

4

ON THE ROAD

Route 66 dates back to the 1920s. It once stretched nearly 2,500 miles (4,023 kilometers) long from Chicago to Los Angeles. Today, Oklahoma maintains one of the longest drivable sections of this historic roadway.

BLUE WHALE OF CATOOSA
ROUTE 66

CENTENNIAL LAND RUN MONUMENT

NATIONAL WEATHER CENTER

OKLAHOMA CITY ZOO

WICHITA MOUNTAINS NATIONAL WILDLIFE REFUGE

Soon, the family reaches the Arcadia Round Barn. This 1898 wooden structure is the most photographed landmark on Route 66! Before long, a giant soda pop bottle invites the family to POPS. This Arcadia restaurant offers 700 flavors of soda. Welcome to Oklahoma!

COLORADO

Oklahoma lies in the south-central United States. It is about halfway between the east and west coasts. The saucepan-shaped state covers 69,899 square miles (181,038 square kilometers). The northwestern panhandle is a narrow strip of land that touches New Mexico to the west. Colorado and Kansas lie to the north. Missouri and Arkansas are Oklahoma's eastern neighbors. Texas borders Oklahoma to the south and west. The Red River flows along much of the southern border.

Oklahoma City is the capital and largest city. It sits in the center of the state. Other major cities include Tulsa, Norman, and Broken Arrow.

NEW MEXICO

KANSAS

MISSOURI

OKLAHOMA

TULSA

BROKEN
ARROW

EDMOND

OKLAHOMA CITY

NORMAN

LAWTON

RED
RIVER

TEXAS

ARKANSAS

OKLAHOMA
LAND RUN

THE SOONERS

The Oklahoma Land Run was set for noon on April 22, 1889. But some settlers snuck into the area sooner to claim the best land. That is how Oklahoma became known as the Sooner State.

Hunters followed herds of bison into Oklahoma more than 10,000 years ago. Over time, they formed many tribes that built villages and grew crops. In 1541, European explorers reached Oklahoma. It became part of the United States through the **Louisiana Purchase** in 1803.

THE LOUISIANA PURCHASE

In the 1830s, the U.S. government forced many Native Americans to move from the southeastern U.S. to Oklahoma. Thousands died during this journey known as the **Trail of Tears**. The government opened Oklahoma to **settlers** in the late 1800s. Newcomers flooded into the area. In 1907, Oklahoma became the 46th state.

NATIVE PEOPLES OF OKLAHOMA

CHEROKEE NATION

- Original lands in Georgia, Tennessee, North Carolina, and South Carolina
- Many were forced into Alabama in the 1700s
- More than 240,000 in Oklahoma today

CREEK NATION

- Original lands in Alabama and Georgia
- Around 65,070 in Oklahoma today
- Also called the Muscogee

CHOCTAW NATION

- Original lands in Mississippi
- Around 85,000 in Oklahoma today

Most of Oklahoma is flat **plains**. The High Plains cover the panhandle. The region's flat-topped Black **Mesa** is the state's highest point. The land gradually lowers to the Red Bed Plains in central Oklahoma. In the northeast, streams flow through steep valleys in the Ozark **Plateau**.

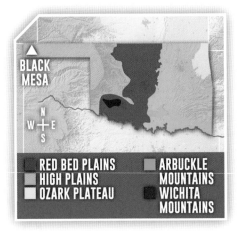

BLACK MESA

N
W + E
S

■ RED BED PLAINS	■ ARBUCKLE MOUNTAINS	
■ HIGH PLAINS		
■ OZARK PLATEAU	■ WICHITA MOUNTAINS	

Several low, forested ridges run east to west on the eastern border. Wetlands and farmland spread along the Red River in the southeast. The Arbuckle and Wichita Mountains stand in the south.

TURNER FALLS
ARBUCKLE MOUNTAINS

SPRING
HIGH: 71°F (22°C)
LOW: 49°F (9°C)

SUMMER
HIGH: 92°F (33°C)
LOW: 70°F (21°C)

FALL
HIGH: 73°F (23°C)
LOW: 51°F (11°C)

WINTER
HIGH: 53°F (12°C)
LOW: 32°F (0°C)

°F = degrees Fahrenheit
°C = degrees Celsius

Oklahoma has hot summers. Strong thunderstorms and tornadoes can strike this time of year. Winters are mild, but ice storms can pose a danger.

NINE-BANDED ARMADILLO

Oklahoma's grassy plains are home to many animals. Armadillos, woodchucks, and moles dig underground tunnels. Prairie dogs pop out of their **burrows**. Kingsnakes and rattlesnakes hide in grasses and rocks. Bison roam around protected lands. Roadrunners chase lizards and scorpions. Scissor-tail flycatchers soar high above the land.

SPECKLED KINGSNAKE

The state's forests shelter raccoons, opossums, and foxes. Red-headed woodpeckers, blue jays, and northern mockingbirds perch in branches. Deer dash between the trees. Trout, bass, and catfish swim in Oklahoma's rivers and lakes.

RED FOX

SCISSOR-TAIL FLYCATCHER

RED-HEADED WOODPECKER

SELMAN BAT CAVE

More than a million Mexican free-tailed bats return from Mexico to Oklahoma's Selman Bat Cave every summer.

AMERICAN BISON

Life Span: up to 20 years
Status: near threatened

American bison range =

LEAST CONCERN	NEAR THREATENED	VULNERABLE	ENDANGERED	CRITICALLY ENDANGERED	EXTINCT IN THE WILD	EXTINCT

Nearly 4 million people live in Oklahoma. Large cities are home to about two of every three residents. Others live in small cities and **rural** communities.

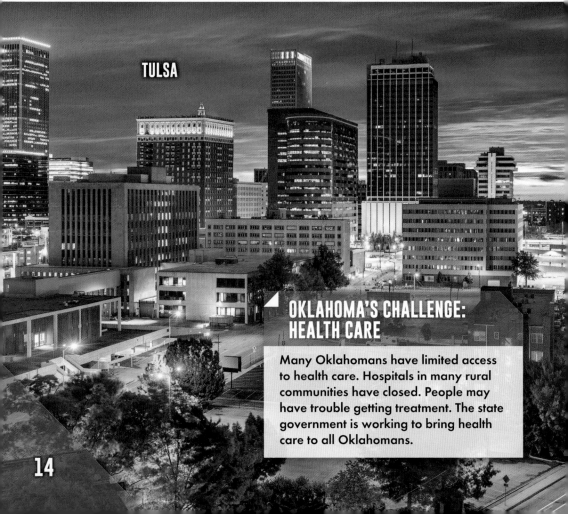

TULSA

OKLAHOMA'S CHALLENGE: HEALTH CARE

Many Oklahomans have limited access to health care. Hospitals in many rural communities have closed. People may have trouble getting treatment. The state government is working to bring health care to all Oklahomans.

FAMOUS OKLAHOMAN

Name: Wilma Mankiller
Born: November 18, 1945
Died: April 6, 2010
Hometown: Tahlequah, Oklahoma
Famous For: Native American rights activist who served as the first female chief of the Cherokee Nation

About 3 out of 4 Oklahomans have **ancestors** from Europe. They arrived in the 1800s. The state has one of the largest Native American populations in the country. About 1 of every 10 Oklahomans is Native American. Hispanic people make up the fastest-growing population. Smaller numbers of Black or African Americans and Asian Americans live in the state. Recent **immigrants** come from Mexico, Vietnam, India, Germany, and Guatemala.

15

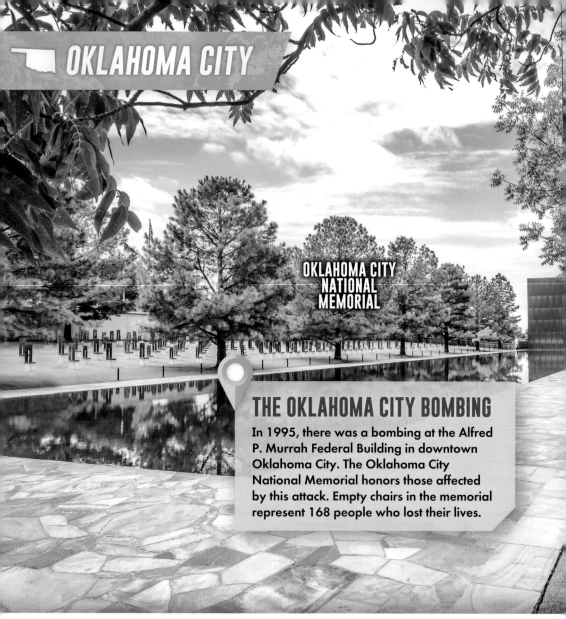

OKLAHOMA CITY NATIONAL MEMORIAL

THE OKLAHOMA CITY BOMBING

In 1995, there was a bombing at the Alfred P. Murrah Federal Building in downtown Oklahoma City. The Oklahoma City National Memorial honors those affected by this attack. Empty chairs in the memorial represent 168 people who lost their lives.

Oklahoma City grew around a train stop near the North Canadian River. The settlement grew during the Oklahoma Land Run of 1889. Oklahoma City became the state capital in 1910. Today, it is the state's largest city and a center for oil production. Tinker Air Force Base is one of the largest employers.

Residents head downtown to shops and restaurants in Bricktown. They explore galleries in the Paseo Arts District. Community theaters and the Oklahoma City Philharmonic draw big audiences. The Myriad **Botanical Gardens** is a popular park. Nearly 2,000 animals bring visitors to the Oklahoma City Zoo.

MYRIAD BOTANICAL GARDENS

BRICKTOWN

OKLAHOMA'S CHALLENGE: EARTHQUAKES AND THE ENVIRONMENT

Oil and gas companies force wastewater deep underground to get rid of it. This process can cause earthquakes that pollute Oklahoma's water supply. Oklahoma's government must work with oil and gas companies to help protect the environment.

Most Oklahomans have **service jobs**. Many work in hospitals, banks, and restaurants. The energy industry also employs many people. Companies produce oil, natural gas, and wind energy. Other workers mine coal, limestone, and salt. Helium and iodine are also important **natural resources**. Oklahoma is the only state that produces iodine!

Farmland stretches across much of the state. The rich soil is ideal for growing wheat, corn, and rye. Other important crops include cotton, pecans, and soybeans. Ranchers raise beef cattle and horses. Factory workers make machinery and metal products.

INVENTED IN OKLAHOMA

YIELD SIGN
Date Invented: 1950
Inventor: Clinton Riggs

PARKING METER
Date Invented: 1935
Inventor: Carl Magee

VOICEMAIL
Date Invented: 1970s
Inventor: Gordon Matthews

SHOPPING CART
Date Invented: 1937
Inventors: Sylvan Goldman and Fred Young

19

BARBECUED PORK

Oklahoma has an official state meal! It includes barbecued pork, chicken-fried steak, and sausage with biscuits and gravy. Corn bread, grits, and black-eyed peas are served on the side. Other side dishes feature fried okra, fried squash, and corn. The meal ends with strawberries and pecan pie for dessert.

Fry bread tacos made with beans, chili, tomatoes, and cheese are popular at powwows. Onion burgers mix beef with onions and are served on a bun. Families ate them during the Great Depression when meat was scarce. Fried pies were a favorite cowboy treat. These fruit-filled pastries are still popular today.

FRY BREAD TACO

EASY FRIED PIE

20 SERVINGS

Have an adult help you make this tasty dessert!

INGREDIENTS

4 6-ounce tubes refrigerated biscuits

Flour for rolling out biscuits

1 cup canola oil

1 20-ounce can fruit pie filling, any flavor

Powdered sugar for dusting

DIRECTIONS

1. Remove the biscuits from the packages, and let stand at room temperature for 20 minutes.

2. On a lightly floured surface, roll out each biscuit to about 4 to 5 inches (10 to 13 centimeters) long.

3. Add 2 tablespoons of pie filling to the middle of each biscuit. Fold the dough over the filling, and seal the edges with a fork.

4. Heat the oil in a pan, and carefully add 2 to 3 pies at a time.

5. Cook for about 8 to 10 seconds on each side or until golden brown.

6. Remove the biscuits from the oil, and place them on a paper towel to drain.

7. Dust with powdered sugar and enjoy!

RODEO

Oklahomans are huge sports fans. High school football games become community gatherings on Friday nights. College football fans fill the stands for the Sooners football team from the University of Oklahoma. Basketball fans cheer for the Oklahoma State Cowboys. They also follow the state's professional basketball team, the Oklahoma City Thunder. Riding and roping events draw big crowds to rodeo arenas.

Oklahomans enjoy swimming, boating, and fishing in the state's lakes and rivers. Hikers and horseback riders follow winding trails through forests. Adventure-lovers go rock climbing and explore caves. The state's theaters, art museums, and concert halls are also popular.

THE STATE SONG

The song "Oklahoma!" from the Broadway musical *Oklahoma!* became the official state song in 1953. The musical takes place in 1906 before Oklahoma was a state.

NOTABLE SPORTS TEAM

Oklahoma City Thunder
Sport: National Basketball Association
Started: 2008
Place of Play: Chesapeake Energy Arena

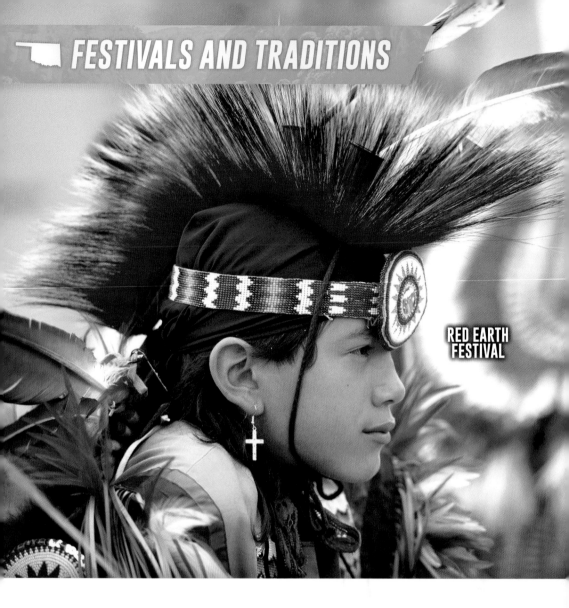

RED EARTH
FESTIVAL

Many of Oklahoma's festivals reflect its Native American and **pioneer** roots. At the Red Earth Festival in Oklahoma City each June, Native American artists display their work. A powwow features thousands of dancers in **traditional** dress. Every April, the 89er Day Celebration remembers the Oklahoma Land Run of 1889. Celebrated in various cities, it includes carnivals and parades.

Oklahomans celebrate spring with the Azalea Festival in April. More than 30,000 azaleas bloom in Muskogee's Honor Heights Park. Oklahoma City hosts the State Fair every September. Oklahomans gather to celebrate what makes their state great!

OKLAHOMA STATE FAIR

AZALEA FESTIVAL

1541

Francisco Vásquez de Coronado is the first European to explore Oklahoma

1889

White settlers rush to claim land in parts of Oklahoma when the U.S. government opens the territory for settlement

1830s

The U.S. government forces thousands of Native Americans to move to Indian Territory in Oklahoma

1803

The United States gains Oklahoma in the Louisiana Purchase

1867

Cowboys begin to drive cattle through Oklahoma to Kansas

1995

A national terrorist bombs the Alfred P. Murrah Federal Building in Oklahoma City, causing 168 people to lose their lives

1907

Oklahoma becomes the 46th state

1930s

Thousands of Oklahomans move west in search of relief from a severe drought known as the Dust Bowl

1897

Oklahoma's first commercial oil well is drilled in Bartlesville

2013

A powerful tornado in Moore takes the lives of 24 people and destroys hundreds of homes and businesses

Nicknames: The Sooner State, The Panhandle State

State Motto: *Labor Omnia Vincit*
(Labor Conquers All Things)

Date of Statehood: November 16, 1907
(the 46th state)

Capital City: Oklahoma City ★

Other Major Cities: Tulsa, Norman, Broken Arrow, Lawton, Edmond

Area: 69,899 square miles (181,038 square kilometers); Oklahoma is the 20th largest state.

Population

3,959,353
(2020)

STATE FLAG

OKLAHOMA

Oklahoma adopted its state flag in 1925. The flag features an Osage warrior's shield decorated with seven eagle feathers. Small crosses on the shield represent goals to strive toward. The olive branch and Plains Indian-style peace pipe are symbols of peace between white people and Native Americans. The state name lies below the shield. The blue background stands for loyalty.

INDUSTRY

JOBS

- MANUFACTURING **6%**
- FARMING AND NATURAL RESOURCES **10%**
- GOVERNMENT **16%**
- SERVICES **68%**

Main Exports

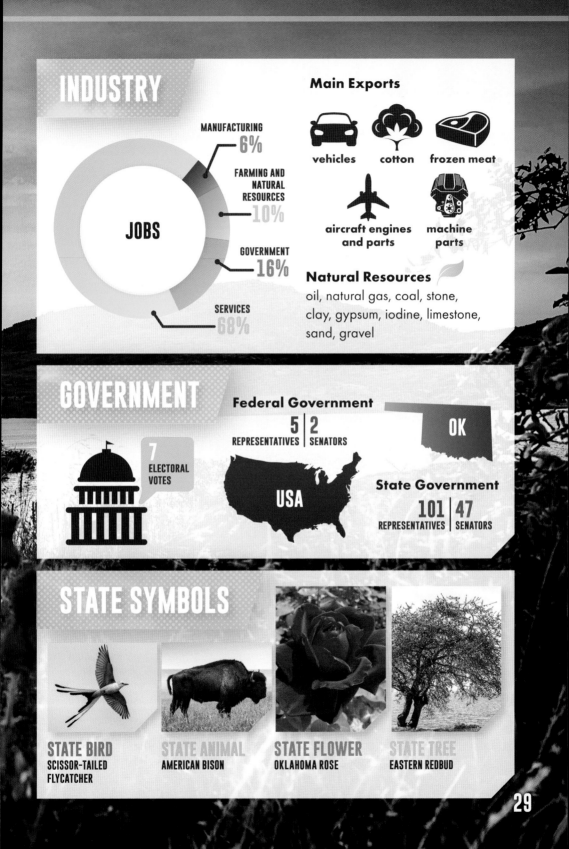

vehicles

cotton

frozen meat

aircraft engines and parts

machine parts

Natural Resources

oil, natural gas, coal, stone, clay, gypsum, iodine, limestone, sand, gravel

GOVERNMENT

Federal Government

5 REPRESENTATIVES | **2** SENATORS

OK

7 ELECTORAL VOTES

USA

State Government

101 REPRESENTATIVES | **47** SENATORS

STATE SYMBOLS

STATE BIRD
SCISSOR-TAILED FLYCATCHER

STATE ANIMAL
AMERICAN BISON

STATE FLOWER
OKLAHOMA ROSE

STATE TREE
EASTERN REDBUD

GLOSSARY

ancestors—relatives who lived long ago

botanical gardens—large, usually public gardens where plants are grown in order to be studied

burrows—holes animals make in the ground

fry bread—a Native American flatbread made from frying dough

Great Depression—a period of worldwide economic crisis that began in 1929 and lasted throughout the 1930s; many Americans did not have jobs during the Great Depression.

immigrants—people who move to a new country

Louisiana Purchase—a deal made between France and the United States; it gave the United States 828,000 square miles (2,144,510 square kilometers) of land west of the Mississippi River.

mesa—a flat-topped hill

natural resources—materials in the earth that are taken out and used to make products or fuel

pioneer—related to a person who is among the first to explore or settle an area

plains—large areas of flat land

plateau—an area of flat, raised land

powwows—Native American gatherings that usually include dancing

rural—related to the countryside

service jobs—jobs that perform tasks for people or businesses

settlers—people who move to live in a new, undeveloped region

totem pole—a tall pole that is painted or carved with symbols for a family or tribe, especially among Native Americans

traditional—related to customs, ideas, or beliefs handed down from one generation to the next

Trail of Tears—the forced relocation of up to 100,000 Native Americans from their homelands to areas farther west in the 1830s

TO LEARN MORE

AT THE LIBRARY

Decker, Michael. *US Route 66*. Minneapolis, Minn.: Abdo Publishing, 2020.

Hesse, Karen. *Out of the Dust*. New York, N.Y.: Scholastic Press, 1997.

Orr, Tamra B. *Oklahoma*. New York, N.Y.: Children's Press, 2018.

ON THE WEB

FACTSURFER

Factsurfer.com gives you a safe, fun way to find more information.

1. Go to www.factsurfer.com.

2. Enter "Oklahoma" into the search box and click Q.

3. Select your book cover to see a list of related content.

31

INDEX